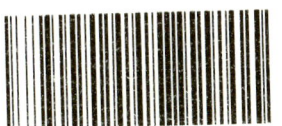

Les Âmes Qui Brûlent

The Burning Souls

Les Âmes Qui Brûlent

The Burning Souls

also known as *Militia*

A poetic memoir of

— Léon Degrelle —

Translated by Rollo of Gaunt

Antelope Hill Publishing

Copyright © Antelope Hill Publishing 2020

All rights reserved.
Originally published in French, A la Feuille de Chêne, 1964
First English printing 2020.

Translated by Rollo of Gaunt

Cover art by sswifty

The publisher can be contacted at
Antelopehillpublishing.com

Hardcover ISBN-13: 978-1-953730-45-9

Translator's Note

This edition of Léon Degrelle's *The Burning Souls* is intended for the English reader, for whom there has thus far been no reliable translation of this particular work. This work has been a labor of love, and so while I am not the most qualified man to produce such a translation, I have faith that those more linguistically skilled than myself will forgive me for any errors, and if I inspire any of them to produce a better version, so much the better.

The Burning Souls is half-prose, half-poetic, and as such, I have attempted throughout to preserve Degrelle's meanings and intentions to the best of my ability, and also to preserve the impassioned quality with which he spoke and wrote throughout his lifetime. I hope only that I have done some justice to the author's depth of emotion.

May this man who found little rest in life find rest in what lies beyond, and may all men who grow weary and lose hope be inspired by his steadfast determination and unwavering courage in the face of great tragedy.

Rollo of Gaunt

Contents

Part One: Empty Hearts 1
    I – The Flame and the Ashes 3
    II – The Agony of the Century 9
    III – The Right Path 12

Part Two: Wellsprings of Life 17
    IV – The Land of Our Birth 19
    V – Hearth and Stone 20
    VI – The Breath of Life 24
    VII – The Task of Happiness 27
    VIII – Christmastime 29

Part Three: The Misery of Mankind 35
    IX – The Blind Men 37
    X – The Lines of Sorrow 38
    XI – The Saints 40
    XII – The Eternal Crucifixion 41
    XIII – Nobody 43
    XIV – To Have Loved 46

Part Four: The Joy of Mankind 51
    XV – Strong and Hard 53
    XVI – The Price of Life 55
    XVII – Despoliation 56
    XVIII – The Power of Joy 57

- XIX – To Dream, to Think 58
- XX – Patience 60
- XXI – Obedience 60
- XXII – Kindness 62
- XXIII – Happy Isolation 62
- XXIV – Grandeur 65

Part Five: A Man's Duty 69
- XXV – The Great Retreat 71
- XXVI – The Taming of Horses 76
- XXVII – The Apocalyptic Cycle 80
- XXVIII – Enlightenment 83
- XXIX – Intransigence 87
- XXX – The Cross 90

Part Six: To Give Completely 97
- XXXI – The Reconquest 99
- XXXII – Flotilla of Souls 101
- XXXIII – Summits 105

Their soul will contain what hers has contained.

The images of her heart will trace great reflections on them, like shadows advancing in the fields under the white clouds of the great summer sky.

She can only bear their gaze if her soul is as clear as theirs.

All that is not fresh and pure astonishes children and leaves a mark on their hearts.

They will not receive strength and renunciation, wisdom and simplicity, virtue and joy, unless their spiritual nourishment is as pure as mother's milk.

The faces of mothers are noble, supremely clear, rejuvenated by the presence of willfully innocent lives even through a thousand days of hardship.

Women are greatly blessed by the body that trembles, turned towards the inner dream, in which dwells the grand secret of the breath of life.

VII – The Task of Happiness

The more we walk among false smiles, greedy or unclean eyes, grasping hands, withered bodies, the more we are disappointed by the mediocrity of existence.

We quickly realize that only the joys put in our hearts when we were young remain solid and eternal. It is in youth that we are made happy or unhappy forever.

If we had a calm childhood, soft as a big golden sky, if we learned to love and to give of ourselves, if we enjoyed, when we were very young, the enchantment that the sky and the light gave us at all times, nature always within our reach and always changing, if we were made with a simple heart, naive as the morning, human, sensitive, good, linked to real and natural affections, then life will remain for us until the end of our troubled days like the sky arrayed powerful and clear over even the most treacherous roads.

There is a task to happiness.

We either develop it or suffocate it.

If we train children, simply, in deep but elementary joys, they will advance in life by keeping in their eyes the light of their inner life, balanced, persevering.

But if we ruin their childhood, if they have seen too much or heard too much, if they have been caught in a whirlwind, if years of calm tenderness have not strengthened in them the tender happiness of their innocence, then their life will be what their childhood was: witnessing disorder, they will become disordered. Having never been made steady in their tastes, their feelings, their thoughts, they will be at the mercy of the winds, possessing only illusory joys that will burn them and immiserate them at the whims of others.

It becomes far more difficult to change later.

A hardened tree cannot be straightened; one can at most clear the foliage or cut back branches.

But when it was young, full of sap, we could have

straightened it with an agile finger, guided it, helped it to flourish.

It is at a time when children simply seem to be playing, watching, simply observing a sparrow or a lark, spelling words and giving kisses, that they photograph in their hearts, in their imagination, exactly that which we give them.

Life is just the development of this photography; the acids of existence will imprint on them the images, beautiful and powerful, or troubled and sad, which we have offered to their curious little eyes, to their clear hearts like sheets of shiny paper.

What we deprive them of by our pride or our agitation, or, alas, by our passions, will be cruelly repaid to us in seeing them unstable, dissatisfied, the soul weakened or ravaged by our own fault.

VIII – Christmastime

We were only little children from the Ardennes.

The snow blanketed the horizon, piled above the eaves of the roofs, and packed itself tight into the bottoms of our shoes.

We were sure we saw Saint Joseph turn around the corner of the Rue du Moulin. To climb the way to the church was tough going in the midnight darkness. At the last steep slope, we resorted to carrying our shoes in our hands. Suddenly, the night of frozen darts gave way to the warm smell of the dazzling naves.

Our heads were spinning a bit.

The smell of the incense intoxicated.

The priest himself was pale.

But from behind the choir-screen came a roar powerful enough to drive away the wild boars ten kilometers from our tangled woods.

The organist pedaled as if he feared arriving late.

The director brought the choir to a wild turbulence.

By the time of "Midnight, Christians," the emotion and the noise had been such that we were climbing atop the straw of the chairs, expecting to see the angels suddenly appear above the choir.

But the angels had continued to stand quietly among the candles, with their large wings at rest.

We approached them, hands clasped under our big woolen gloves. We were kneeling on the marble. The brown ox and the gray donkey were close by. We were burning to touch them, to see if their hair would part like a fountain of water.

But we children loved other children even more than we loved animals. Jesus was lying on the straw. It softened our hearts to think he must be cold. Nobody had given him thick stockings like us. No shoes. No scarf to wrap across his nose. No green woolen gloves to cover his hands. We looked a little astonished at the father Saint Joseph, who

Part One:

— Empty Hearts —

I – The Flame and the Ashes

Here I am, nearly at the end of my life. I felt almost everything. Knew everything. More than anything, I suffered.

I saw, dazzled, the great golden fires of my youth arise. Their flames illuminated my land. The crowds made the starry waves of their thousands of faces dance around me. Their fervor, their eddies existed.

But did they really, in fact, exist? Wasn't all this a dream? Did I not dream that thirty years ago, a nation called my name, and that on certain days the most distant newspapers of the planet repeated it?

Tucked away in my exiled sadness, I can no longer believe in my past itself. Did I live those times or not? Know those passions? Raise those oceans? I walk my terraces. I lean over my roses. I discern the scents. Have I ever been another being, other than this lonely dreamer who vainly clutches at memories frayed like mountain fogs?

Wasn't all this something other than a hallucination?

I cannot see, far away, far away, in faded lights, their bodies, as if from a Greco painting, growing thinner and thinner. Did these men who have faded forever from the horizon know me? Did they follow me? Did I lead them? Did I exist?

In my memories, as in my hands, I no longer feel that fleeting wind. My eyes—and what eyes should I have, eyes of desperation? — my eyes may search the impassive sky, try to see in the depths of the years, in the depths of the century, what did it mean?

The being that I am, in what way is it still the being that once carried my name, who was known, who was listened to? For whom many have lived and for whom alas many have died? This being, what does it have to do with the man who walks, bitter, endlessly alone, upon a few meters of foreign land, rummaging through his past, losing himself in it, no longer believing in it, wondering if it is really he who was tossed a hundred times in the tornadoes of an implacable Destiny, or if this was no more than a dream?

So if I doubt my flesh, my bones, what my public action once forged, if I doubt the reality of my past and the part that I took in a few years of building up the history of men, what can I still believe of the ideals which were born in me, which burned within me, which I projected, of the value of my convictions at the time, of my feelings, of what I thought of humanity, what I dreamed of creating for her?

Each human being is a succession of human beings, as dissimilar from each other as the passers-by whose disparate faces we scrutinize in the street.

At fifty, how do we still look like the young man of twenty whom we are trying to remember and whose survival we want at all costs? Even his flesh is no longer the same flesh; it is gone, has been remade, renewed. No more than a millimeter of skin is the skin of those times.

What then about the soul? And our thoughts? The feelings that propelled us to action? And the feelings that passed to us, like breaths of fire through the heart?

How many distinct men do we carry within us, who fight, who contradict each other, or who even ignore each other? We are good and we are evil, we are the abjection and the dream. We are both, tangled in inextricable nets. But it is not here that the horror of fate lies. The atrocious thing is to break these nets themselves, to throw your soul overboard; the horrible thing is to have to say that the essential in our lives was caricatured, disfigured by a thousand defilements and a thousand denials.

Who has not experienced these debacles?

Some realize their bankruptcy with pain. Others make the observation with cynicism, or with the arrogant smile of those who no longer listen, who are convinced that the knowledge of man and the superiority of the spirit consist in engaging in all "experiences," deliberately exhausting the most perverse pleasures, without excessive astonishment and without regret, having found, in the use and in the desecration of everything, information, the condescension and indifference of an "ethics" of decomposition, free from any spiritual counterbalance.

Without a doubt, the world in which we live has become, to a great extent, the world of these amoral people, so sure of themselves. No doubt, those who would persist in imagining a humanity of high virtues may fancy them to be anachronistic beings, non-evolved, glued to old fads, living apart from men, apart from their time, apart from fashion, apart from reality.

It was here that I arrived. I had dreamed of a century of

Knights, strong and noble, all-dominating. Hard and pure, my banners said. I feel unbalanced, with my bundle of old dreams. I know that feelings like the ones I have tried to express can hardly be felt anymore, or even seem "painful" to some.

But I have seen so much, I have suffered so much that one more bitter thought will not tire me beyond my ability. So, too bad! These dreams, well yes, I had them. These impulses, yes, I carried them. This love of others, yes, it burned within me, it consumed me. I wanted to see in man a heart to love, to excite, to raise, a soul which, even if it was half-asphyxiated by the pestilence of its slavery, aspired to find a pure breath and sometimes only waited for a word, or a look, to emerge and to be reborn.

Let us be straightforward. The right to interject, to use others, the right to moral or spiritual consideration, these I do not have. I know this only too well. I have had my share of miseries, alas, like so many others; and even if I hadn't suffered them myself, I've been loaned so many miseries from others that I can only feel, when I analyze myself, confusion and unfathomable sadness. Yet the spirit of the ideal that throws its fire into this book has devoured me every day of my existence. I should, of course, have left it to others, less affected, the care and responsibility of returning light and song to mankind. But that fire was burning me down. Today, suffocated by a relentless spell, the great fire of yesteryear leaves nothing but ashes. I come back to it anyway, stubbornly, because these ashes evoke the moments of fervor in my life, the deepest impulses, the very spiritual basis of my action. Here they are, disarrayed, delivered to the wind which will quickly disperse them.

These thoughts, these dreams are all in disorder. I have not made a plan. It is the height. I did not sit at my table like a distinguished and reasonable writer. I have not written a "Manual of the Idealist," chapter by chapter, calculating everything, measuring everything. Not that, nothing like that.

What to do!

The impulses of the soul are not graduated like the flow of a gas appliance. Hope, passion, love, faith, pain, and shame dictated to me the writings that I tossed about, at such and such a time, because I felt them then with great force. Sometimes it was at the summit of my public action. Sometimes it was in the abandonment, the mud, and the cold of my distant life as a suffering soldier in the vastness of the Eastern Front. But the soul that lived these impulses followed a common thread, invisible to many: it was nevertheless the artery that spiritually nourished my existence. Therefore, these notes are not so much nonsense, they record the ups and downs of a soul among souls, all of which have their ups and downs.

Certainly, the spirit which has arrived at the stale "wisdom" of cynicism, can dominate by its cold smile, can display the icy marble of its interior tomb and engrave on them its findings with an impassive pen. But fire, it has many forms, it rises, lowers, is reborn, starts anew. This book is fire, with the exaltations of fire, the excess of fire.

If only they could have the beneficent heat! If only the souls could find this comfort and vigor, as we find them meditating in the evening, near a large, almost silent, wood fire! The waves of its powerful life penetrate, and their radiation, and their contemplation. They offer themselves completely, they deliver themselves completely. The gift, the real gift is thus, annihilating until the last brand.

For me—my fire is dead. My life has plunged into the abyss, has been submerged by the black dawn that has smothered everything. But I still want to believe that these impulses, which animated the action of a man already dead in the eyes of most—though he has the misfortune to still live for himself—will still be able to join spiritually from here to there, in the world, anxious hearts.

I remember three words that I had deciphered one day on a tomb of black marble, there in Damme in Flanders, in a church of my lost homeland: ETSI MORTUUS URIT. "Even dead, it burns."

May these pages, the last fleeting fire of what I was, burn for a moment, warm for a moment souls haunted by the passion of giving and believing, believing in spite of everything, in spite of the assurances of the corrupt and the cynics, despite the sad bitter taste that leaves us with the memory of our falls, the awareness of our misery and the immense field of moral ruins of a world that is certain to have no more of salvation, which prides itself on it and which nevertheless must be saved, must more than ever be saved.

Part One: Empty Hearts

II – The Agony of the Century

Love? Why? Why love?

Human beings have barricaded themselves behind their selfishness and pleasure. Virtue has abandoned its natural song. We laugh at our old rites. Souls suffocate. Perhaps they were already liquidated, the evidence hidden behind the decorum of habits and conventions.

Happiness has become, for man and for woman, a heap of fruit which they devour in a hurry, or in which they plant their teeth, without more, and reject them pell-mell – damaged bodies, damaged souls – quickly exhausted by the fleeting frenzy, already looking for other more exciting or more perverse fruits.

The air is charged with all moral and spiritual denials. The lungs draw in vain for a breath of fresh air, the freshness of a spray thrown close to the sands.

Man's interior gardens have lost their colors and their birdsong. Love itself is no longer given. And besides, what is love, the most beautiful word in the world, reduced to the rank of physical pastime, instinctive and interchangeable?

The only happiness lays in the gift, the only happiness that consoles, that intoxicates like the full fragrance of the fruits and leaves of autumn.

Happiness only exists in the gift, the complete gift; his selflessness gives him the flavor of eternity; he returns to the lips of the soul with an intangible sweetness.

Give! To have seen eyes that shine, to have been

understood, touched, fulfilled!

Give! Feel the grand, happy tablecloths, floating like dancing water on a heart suddenly adorned with sun!

Give! To have reached the secret fibers that weave the mysteries of sensibility!

Give! To have this gesture which unburdens the hand, which relieves its carnal weight, which exhausts the need to be loved!

Then the heart becomes as light as pollen. Its pleasure rises like the song of the nightingale, a burning voice that lights the darkness. We pour forth with joy. We have emptied this power of happiness which was not to be partaken selfishly, which encumbered us, which we had to pour out, in the same way that the earth cannot endlessly contain the life of springs and lets them burst under crocuses and daffodils, or in the faults of the green rocks.

But today in a thousand withered wells the springs of life have ceased to flow. The earth no longer pours out this gift which swelled it. She holds back her happiness. She chokes.

The agony of our time lies here. The century does not fail for lack of material support. Never before has the universe been so rich, filled with so much comfort, helped by such productive industrialization. Never have there been so many resources or goods offered. It is the heart of man, and this alone, which is bankrupt. It is by a lack of love, it is by a failure of believing and of giving oneself, that the world has overwhelmed itself with murderous blows.

This century wanted to be no more than the century of appetites. Its pride was wasted. It believed in machines, stocks, and ingots, over which it would be master. It believed, just as much, in the victory of carnal passions projected beyond all limits, in the liberation of the most diverse forms of enjoyment, constantly multiplied, always more degraded and degrading, endowed with a "technique" which is, after all, generally only an accumulation, without great imagination, of rather impoverished vices, of emptied beings.

From his conquests, or more precisely from his mistakes, then from his falls, man acquired pleasures that seemed supremely exciting at first, and which were in fact only poison, filth, and falsehood.

For this falsehood, this filth, and this poison, however, the man and the woman had abandoned, had desecrated, through their dreams and their devastated bodies, inner joy, true joy, the great sun of true joy. The puffs of pleasure from possessions—matter or flesh—must, being illusory, and compounding in their flaws, sooner or later vanish.

What remains is only the passion for taking, seizing, in bouts of anger that set them against all obstacles and against the stale odors of decay clinging to their ransacked and rotten lives.

Vain, emptied, their hands dangling, they do not even see the moment approaching when the artificial work of their time will collapse.

It will collapse because it is contrary to the very laws of the heart, and—let's say the big word—to the laws of God.

He alone, so strong that we laughed at Him, gave the world its balance, directed the passions, opened to us the gates of complete giving and authentic love, gave a meaning to our days, whatever our happiness and our misfortunes.

We can gather all the Conferences of the world, gather by herds the Heads of State, the economic experts and the champions of all the techniques. They will weigh. They will decree. But, essentially, they will fail because they will ignore the obvious.

The disease of the century is not in the body.

The body is sick because the soul is sick.

This is what is essential, whatever it may take to cure.

The real, the great revolution to be made is there.

Spiritual revolution.

Or the ruin of the century.

The salvation of the world is in the will of souls who believe.

III – The Right Path

Those who hesitate in the face of struggle are those whose souls are numb. A grand ideal always gives you the strength to overcome the body, to suffer from fatigue, from hunger, from cold. What matter sleepless nights, overwhelming toil, stress, or poverty! The main thing is to have at the bottom of your heart a great force which warms and which pushes forward, which revives the loose nerves, which makes the tired blood beat with great blows, which puts in the eyes that fire which burns and which conquers.

Then suffering is of no consequence, the pain itself becomes joy because it is a means of enhancing one's legacy, of purifying one's sacrifice.

Ease sedates the ideal. Nothing rights it better than the whip of hard life; it makes us understand the depth of the duties to be assumed, the mission of which we must be worthy.

The rest does not count.

Health does not matter. We are not on earth to eat on time, to sleep on time, to live a hundred years or more. All this is vain and foolish.

Only one thing matters: having a useful life, sharpening your soul, improving it at all times, monitoring your weaknesses and exalting your impulses, serving others, throwing happiness and tenderness around you, giving your arm to your neighbor, to rise all by helping each other. Once these duties are accomplished, what does it mean to die at the age of thirty or a hundred years, to feel the fever throbbing at the hours when the human beast cries out, at the end of its power?

Let him get up again, despite everything!

The ideal appears to give its strength only at the breaking point.

Only the soul counts and must dominate everything

else. Short or long, life is only redeemed if we have no cause for shame at the moment we have to give it back.

When the sweetness of the days calls to us, and the joy of loving, and the beauty of a face, a perfect body, a light sky, and the call of distant races, when we are close to giving in to the lips, to the colors, to the light, to the numbness of the relaxed hours, let us tighten in our hearts all these dreams, on the verge of the golden escape.

The true escape is to quit our dear, sensitive prey, at the very moment when the sweet scent invites our bodies to fail.

At this hour, when you must abandon softness and place love above desire, when everything is painful to the point of cruelty, a sacrifice really begins to be whole, to be pure.

Then we have surpassed ourselves, we are finally giving something. Before, we looked only to ourselves, and the concern for pride and selfish glory corrupted what flowed out from our souls, and it was used, instead of given.

One gives for good, without calculation—because all is given, and nothing remains of the giver—only when one first kills the love of the self. This does not come easily, because the human beast is reluctant. We understand so poorly what can be learned from bitterness.

It is sweet to dream of an ideal and to build it in your mind.

Still, to tell the truth, this is precious little.

What is an ideal if it is just a game, or a sweet dream?

Part One: Empty Hearts

You have to build it, after that, in reality.

Each stone must be torn from our comfort, from our joys, from our rest, from our heart.

When, despite everything, the building rises over the years, when you do not stop along the way, when, faced with heavier and heavier stones to be placed, you continue, only then does the ideal begin to live.

It lives only to the extent that we die to ourselves.

What a drama, deep down, that righteous life.

Part Two:

— Wellsprings of Life —

IV – The Land of Our Birth

As men we belong always to a people, a land, a history. We may not know it. We can try to forget it. But events eternally return us to these sources of life.

They bring us back first to the men of our blood: shameful or bright, family binds us together, ever tighter and firmer with time.

It can even become suffocating. We never get rid of it.

Where our blood is concerned, we are bound to it. Blood comes always before reason. We are one with these ties, as if our veins were only one organism and the family had only one heart, a heart that pumps the same blood in each of us and reminds us of our vital hearth.

The same is true of our homeland.

We cannot escape it.

The sight of a yellowed print of our cathedrals, the memory of the smell of the dunes, of the gray hue of our hillsides, of the curve of our rivers, brings up to our throat a love that stifles us, that makes our voices hoarse.

The country's past is embedded in the depth of our consciousness and our sensibilities.

Everything about us is survival, rebirth, even if unconsciously.

The past of a country is reborn in each generation as

spring returns, always in new sprouts.

We may be unburdened, traverse the world, lose our mind: the native soil still sends into our hearts an essence that we do not create and that dominates us.

All that it takes is the voice of a radio station picked up in a distant country, brought by imprecise waves, so that memories, ties, and laws emerge again, real watermarks indestructibly embedded in the fabric of our tormented days.

V – Hearth and Stone

You must have wandered over the most distant seas, known the red nights of the Tropics, the cane fires, the songs of the negroes, the deserts with their pink sands, their leafless shrubs, the skeletons of horses bleached by the winds, you must have climbed frozen lakes and hot snow, picked mimosa flowers from the ruins of Carthage, grapefruits in Havana, a blade of grass near the fluted pillars of the Acropolis, to fully love your homeland, that which we first saw, with the only lucid eyes in the world: the eyes of a child.

It is necessary to have known other journeys, with furniture and clothes, books, tables, the simple material goods, it is necessary to have been this nomad of the anonymous, apartments where one sits as one sits in a train, to know the passion and the nostalgia of the first of all landscapes, of this place in the heart that is "home."

We can speak without regret of the great joys of foreign

lands. They still gild our eyes: the day rises yellow and silver on the palm trees which skirt the Sea of the Antilles; clouds of fog in the olive trees of the Delphi valley; fishermen rowing in the clear blue night of the Cyclades; the palm grove streaked with sun near the red walls of Marrakech. But the memory of wandering journeys in the prisons of our soulless lodgings weighs us down and suffocates us.

What remains in our life of these impersonal relays?

The walls where we heartlessly hung and removed the paintings? The apartment next door from where you were surveilled? The mingled chatter of telephones? The staircase where we meet without knowing each other? The cell car of the elevator with its double bars?

We look at this decor of life and death with dull eyes, charged with veritable despair.

What do these partitions tell us, the kitchen open to a horrible courtyard, a few meters long, without an unexpected nook, without a quirk, barren of natural foliage, without a cozy nest? What say these beds and furniture, always awkward and embarrassed, as if they feel out of place, poor, unhappy, vaguely nomadic?

Even furniture has a soul.

The old sideboard that clutters the corridor, the clock case that no longer resonates so as not to annoy anyone, once lived, once knew a real house, had for a hundred years, two hundred years, their place, their touch, their scent.

Poor sideboard and poor clock, far from the polished

parquet, from the smell of lavender, the worn and water-stained staircase, the conversation all about, the salute of the sun entering suddenly through an opened door.

We alienated moderns, dragged from apartment to apartment in soulless cities, feel a little more torn from our hearts each time we have to cross a new threshold, light up the sterile white corridors, get used to these handles, these shutters, this door that does not hold, this gas stove that flares up too quickly, these buses that pass by with awful horns that crush the soul.

We are silent.

But we forget nothing.

And man, like the old sideboard and the big clock, motionless, looks and sees.

The land of our birth returns to life in our memories. Here it is. A little foliage lights up the facade. Two blue stone steps. A large vine-encumbered balcony in the gardens. Everything is in its place. Everything has a meaning, a smell, a form. We go to the cupboard: the cupboard, that beautiful, full, serious word because it holds our nourishing bread. So familiar we can navigate it with our eyes closed. This corner smells of tobacco; that one the cat, who always purred in the warmest place. That noise is Father rising from the office chair. The halting footstep is Mother, who, in the dining room, waters her flowers. These rooms are not merely places to stop. This one is the room "above the living room," this one is the room "above the office," this one is the room "of the little ones," even when they have become men with *heavy thoughts*.

Each of these rooms has its history, has known its vigils, its maladies; we left it one morning carrying a darling body in our arms.

Ah! The horror of our children being born or dying in anonymous apartments, surrounded by living furnishings since departed, where other nomads have, in their turn, resumed their awkward life, without soulful memories, not even daring to remember, so out of place are they.

House of yesteryear, with your poor draperies, your occasional bad taste, this ball on the railing, these photos of children *à la queue leu leu*, the grand piano, the black fireplace, the tin bathtub where people washed one after the other, these steps that we still scale twenty years later in memories, the breaths that we hear again passing close to us, the face of the mother who appears, first in the distance, then right there before our eyes, almost inscrutable, we feel like children, desiring again her soft caress.

Calls of immense tenderness rise with distant scents of flowers and foliage; songs of water pass at the bottom of the garden, the soft sunshine filling our entire world.

Everything we are comes from that time. Unfortunate are children who have never had a house of their own, and who do not collect these memories from which our life flows.

It is the home that forms us into who we are.

How can we have a soul in a faceless house, one that is changed like a carnival mask?

Life is fixed on hearth and stone; the rest flows away like

broken wood floating on a winter stream.

Home, our tender fortress.

It takes on a unique face, little by little, built over time, through common hardships and the birth of children.

The walls hold love and dreams.

Its furnishings, beautiful or ugly, are our companions and witnesses.

A sweetness rises slowly from the souls within, it becomes a place of contemplation, rest, and certainty, rather than a brief stop on the journey of our existence.

Softness, balance, points of reference, testimony, self-examination. Without mother and home, tell me, my soul, where would we be?

VI – The Breath of Life

Men can debase themselves, they can live in increasingly frenetic agitation, as millions of madmen engorge themselves—yet the nobility of motherhood preserves, among thousands of natural and vibrant hearts, its own pale radiance. Today, the maternal essence moves just as it did in the days when the first women felt their bodies stirred by its indescribable thrills.

From that hour women are no longer the same. Yesterday they were hurried, their eyes clear, their souls empty, their lips distracted. The life born in them, like a hidden flowering, suddenly gives them gravity, confidence, a great and proud force, the certainty of creating, of giving, and the emotional charm of the living mystery that will one day be born through their pain.

They remain mirthful, but their gaze becomes deeper. They carry within them a treasure whose pulse is intimately linked to their own. Their vigor, their melancholy, this great ideal, sometimes undeclared, which lifts or torments them, thoughts and regrets, joys and desires become one with this hidden life, ever-present for the one who gives it blood and soul in this perfect communion of flesh and heart.

They are brave and weary.

Tired of the overburdened body, of their youth bent like branches laden heavy with fruit, weary of sun and wind.

Yet, still valiant, knowing what renewal their bodies now tenderly contain, in this flesh that their most delicate tremors shape.

They know that this flower-soul, barely open in the night, will bloom tomorrow; the innocent heart which they cover like the night sky is filled with the sweetness and peace of the stars and the silence.

Among the clamorous world they carry this glimmering night.

Their dreamy eyes contemplate these great, moonlit landscapes, where a world known only to them lies dormant, powerful and immense.

They see blue mountains, black and smooth waters, enchanted skies studded with fires, set in the jet-black of evening like ethereal gems.

They advance under these nocturnal lights, the heart taut, but unsure. No one walks beside them. The universe looks elsewhere. They alone watch. They alone have the eyes to see it. They go on, body heavy, soul tense and elevated, as if drawn by the greatness of this secret night.

These months when the flesh blossoms are their private springtime, when only the shadows and the scents, the colors and the lights reach their great love, stretched out with arms open to life, like an orchard of the heart.

They will experience the birth of this new life, sundered from the great dream, then are faced with constant efforts, in the service of these bodies and these souls which enchant them and which frighten them.

Royalty, trembling and radiant.

What will be reborn in these hearts?

Will they keep the song and the purity of mountain waters?

Will these naive eyes ever make you cry? Will this little curly head, the color of the sun on the stone wall, carry good and clear thoughts, the mother's dream, like fiery sword lilies? It is best not to fear too much, to show the straight course, but to leave it lined with greenery and woodlands, and to let them travel, pure and bright, the earthen path to the horizon.

The mother will put in the hearts of the little ones, once again, only what she will have nourished herself.

humbly stood, doing nothing to glorify himself, and the mother clad in blue and white, so still and so beautiful.

We knew only beautiful mothers with pure eyes, in which we saw everything. We had looked into those eyes so often. But those of the Mother of the Little Jesus enchanted us to the extreme, as if Heaven allowed children to see more in them than men did.

We said nothing when going down to the coast.

When children say nothing, it is because they have much to say.

At home, the smoky chocolate and the big table covered with cakes never managed to tear us away, on the return, from invisible conversations between the children of human mothers and the Little Child of the Mother of Heaven.

On the top of the piano, a crib had been erected where we could, standing atop a stool, take the ox and the donkey in our hands.

Little pink and blue candles were lit every night. Each child had their own, on which they would blow a deep breath at the end of the prayers. Behind, kneeling near a chair, in the dark, the mother led our religious impulses, guided us.

When it was all over, when we turned to her in order to obtain the right to put out our little lights, we saw in her two eyes, shining, so much emotional fervor. Paradise comes into the hearts of children through the example of the mother.

At that hour, humble and poignant, the mother knew that little souls had been marked forever, that we could blow out the little candles near the manger, but that they would never be extinguished in our hearts.

Every winter, when Christmas returns, the little flames lit by our mothers once again burn high and bright.

Part Three:

— The Misery of Mankind —

IX – The Blind Men

The money, the honors, the mess of bodies, the eagerness to seize an earthly happiness which leaks between the fingers and always escapes, has made of the human herd a pitiful horde, ruining itself, tearing itself apart to find a liberation which does not exist.

Only the false laughter rising from the rabble serves to remind us that it is not a question of herd animals, but of *men*.

This stampede of the damned seized first the individual, then the people as a whole.

It is no longer a solitary game, in which one is enthralled by personal passions or vices. Whole communities are sucked in by the vertigo of impossible desires, the desire to be the first, that is to say the desire to trample upon, the desire for purely material power, that is to say the desire to suffocate and destroy the spiritual. All willpower, all effort becomes useless in the face of this human dissolution, and it is here that the spiritual always reappears, as a rebuke, or as a curse.

This baseness has poured out from the limited circles of the "elites" into the extended circles of the masses, tossing them about on waves of infinite desire, ambition and pseudo-pleasures which are just caricatures of joy.

The clear water of the heart has been clouded to its outer limits.

The river of men now carries a putrid stink.

The disorder of the century has upset this river that was once light, reeds and plunging flights of swallows.

Men and peoples regard each other with violent eyes, their hands seared and bitten by their avarice.

Every day the world is more selfish and more brutal.

There is great hatred between men, between classes, between peoples, because everyone is bent on the pursuit of material goods which ultimately avail nothing.

But all abandon the goods, proffered to all, of the moral universe and the eternity of the soul.

We run madly, bloody our foreheads beating our heads against the walls, on paths of hatred, or of abjection, or of madness, shouting our passions, throwing ourselves wildly at everything, desiring to gain that which we can never have.

X – The Lines of Sorrow

There are few hearts that have not been soiled with villainy, sordid acts, leprous faults, leaving telltale cracks for those with eyes to see them.

Even hearts washed of the stains of the moral swamp will still keep a bitter taste of imperfection and ashes.

Cracked porcelain can be fixed; yet, whoever saw it broken will forever recognize the lines, however finely repaired, of the break. He knows that the invisible unity of the perfect will never return, but is forever gone.

The longer one lives, the more the heart is marked by these lines of sorrow, imperceptible for all those who have not seen or not known what made them, but heartbreaking by all that they contain of broken delicacy, like fine silks which rend silently.

Happy again, those who are purified by invisible suffering!

How many others, whatever value vice may have, strive to convince themselves that this abasement was useful, forever marked by this burning apparel which has cooled on their skin and sticks to it, corrupts their flesh and becomes one with it.

Whose eyes can one meet without trembling?

What are they hiding?

Who has not been vile one day, who does not carry within himself words, gestures, desires, shameful abdications, or the mummified corpse of his inner life?

How many men, how many women do not even hide the bankruptcy of their senses, their oaths and the miserable desecration of their bodies? Sometimes with remorse. Most of the time, without remorse. Or rather, even with a touch of triumph and insolent provocation.

In the final account, those who have liquidated everything, decency, modesty, respect for oneself, for one's body, for one's word, and God with the rest, are only the result of hundreds of smaller prior denials, denied or hidden from the start.

The whole is destroyed only when the innumerable fibers of the heart have been sheared one after the other by lies and ill-intent, followed by multiple abandonments more and more irremediable, with the conscience assassinated, at the end — disaster.

Decay saps the mind before spreading throughout the whole being.

The body does not yield, does not allow itself to be debased, trapped, and defiled to death until long after the soul, negligent or intoxicated by the appeal of sin, has abandoned the oars which, at the beginning, traced straight paths on pure waters.

XI – The Saints

The Saints, varying in intelligence but possessing a heart given without limits, whom the fallen and corrupt hold in such esteem, the Saints show us that perfection is open to all. They too were simple men, simple women, charged with passions, weaknesses, and often faults.

They too sometimes did to tire, give in, and tell themselves that they would never be able to get rid of that smell of muck and sin that accompanies us.

But still they did not renounce themselves.

With each fall they straightened up, determined to be all

the more vigilant as their strength failed them.

Virtue is not a sudden dazzle but a slow, hard and sometimes very painful conquest. They had the superhuman joy of finally feeling victorious over their bodies and their thoughts.

Their struggle tells us that happiness, on earth and beyond the earth, is within everyone's reach. Every one of us has a choice to make.

Before the body fails, it is the spirit that triumphs or capitulates. And even when the body has given way, the spirit can lift it up, or let it corrupt itself even more, then poison itself forever.

We are our own masters. We can sink into the chasms, or stand in them up to the shoulder, or climb out of them, and overcome them. Everything can be avoided, and everything can be done.

XII – The Eternal Crucifixion

Faced with the contemptuous ironies of hedonists and skeptics, one hardly dares to recall that, for two thousand years, the greatest human drama, that of the Passion, has been spiritually repeated each spring.

Who will suffer, who will be there near Calvary in these new days of agony?

In the desert of time stands the Cross.

The mundane, shady, or perverse life of men flows on

like a dull river. Christ will receive the blows and the thorns. He will collapse to the ground. The wood of the cross will crush His flesh. The hammer will strike great blows against the hard beams. *They pierced my hands and my feet; I can count all my bones.*

What will the world know?

His Blood will slowly come down on His pale Body. His eyes will seek both His Father and our souls.

What will our souls understand about this tragedy?

They have not shuddered or cried.

Nor even thought about it.

Nor seen.

Christ moves well alone. Alone.

The souls sleep, or are sterile, or have committed suicide, while it is to pull them out of their torpor, mud, and death that this Body hangs between Heaven and earth in pain.

The distress of this Heart vainly launches a cry of despair which should freeze the earth and stop the breath of men.

Yet it is because of man's spiritual suffocation that the world is falling apart.

It is hope, charity, justice, humility that the world needs to find fresh air.

We have received this spiritual life as a gift.

We are the bearers.

And our hands are dangling at our sides. And our eyes are dry. And our lips do not tremble in fervor and emotion.

Our hearts are like dry sand.

Our souls lay lifeless where they died.

Faith is only worth anything as long as it conquers, love as long as it burns, charity as long as it saves.

XIII – Nobody

A palm tree trembles. The sand slides between the tanned fingers of a child. Lambs marked with blood collide with stubborn little foreheads. Tiny donkeys, eyes wet, come down from the hill. The Easter landscape, clean and shiny. The air is still fresh. Daisies are scattered on the hillside.

Why does Christ again suffer the most heartbreaking agony in these days when fans of mimosa flowers decorate the twisting roads?

These clear, warm roads bring Him back every year, silent and in agony, to the nails and thorns, to the blood and sputum.

Lord, we are following you in your dusty procession, mingled with those rough and cowardly fishermen who loved you, but who loved you like us: with measure, as if measure was not an insult to your love.

We are like unto them, no worse than others, our eyes sometimes beaming with joy in serving you. We dismiss intruders, we wave the palms, we believe we are very close to your heart: we think ourselves better than we are.

In your sad eyes, it is our vanity that we project.

And in this hour of agony, because our love hung always by a thread, we will turn away from your wounds, your blood and sweat, and that great icy cry that will pierce the earth.

Lord, we're coming back to your blued feet. We clasp this wood of the Cross between our trembling arms.

How dare we look up at your bloody head?

We dare do nothing but extend our dismayed hearts to you. It would have been so sweet to give our souls to you in a complete act, to be with you from the Garden of Olives to this mound where you hang inert in the evening wind. We did not even have the fate of the Penitent Thief, the one who loved you last, who regarded you as he fell into Heaven.

We suffer the overwhelming force of our weaknesses, our cowardice, our tepidity. Lord, you brought us the essential and the eternal, the bread and the wine, the breath and the sun. You animated our hearts; you gave us strength. We should have jumped, lightly, with heart in celebration, freed forever from all bond, all regret, all other hope. Yet we remained, fearful, hidden in the shadow of a doorway or under a bright olive tree. You went, crushed and overwhelmed with insults. Ah! my God! In these minutes of pain and salvation we have not grasped the Cross, we have not kissed your wounds and your thorns, put to flight your executioners, broken their whips, refuted their insults. We did not know how to love.

At the moment of this complete giving, our hearts were lifeless.

My God, there you are abandoned by all, silent and dismal, stiff-limbed. There was nobody, nobody.

We squeeze the dead wood and depart, without raising our heads, laying our defeated hearts at your feet.

You will return to the light, Lord. At this hour, have mercy on the destroyed souls! Have mercy on empty souls!

We suffer so much from our mean and vile sentiments, so imbued with ourselves, so preoccupied with our selfishness, our ambitions, our vanities.

We let you suffer, we saw your blood flow, saw you plant your cross, saw the life fade from your face. Will we ever dare to look upon your open wounds and to meet your weary eyes?

Lord, the hour is near, your light will suddenly burst forth upon the hill. We will still be there, ashamed and sad. Burn our hearts with your dazzling sweetness, give us the warmth and purity of this divine fire from which you will spring.

We are overwhelmed at the threshold of your tomb.

Lord, make the spark of the resurrection bloom in our defeated souls!

XIV – To Have Loved

In the icy, pale gold sky, a lark quivered.

What was she thinking up there?

She shuddered, she uttered strident cries, swooning every second, clinging to the sky with a flutter of wings that passed like a lightning bolt.

She loved to love, until broken, broken with happiness, she fell like a pebble in a furrow

So does the soul soar.

She cries of love. She remains, suspended in mystical immensity, only by the wonder of invisible wings that support her.

She no longer even knows that she can fall, that the ground is under her; she is there, detached from everything, trembling, pulsating, as if speaking!

The lark swooning upon the warm earth must also feel this great joy of fulfilled love. The soul is panting. Love returns in waves and breaks into effort, giving, and joy.

The great tragedy of sin, what causes so much suffering, is that on account of it we give less of ourselves, or give badly, offering only a portion of what we might have, a portion with hints of indelible defilement.

To love is to give. And to give is to give everything. The punishment for falling is the pain of having trampled on your love, of having reduced the love you might have given.

If only we could remove from our bodies, our hands, our eyes, those forces that pulsed in them at the hours of weakness and abjection.

Too late: much to our chagrin.

We may cry all the tears in the world. No matter what, we can never recover that which we so carelessly lost. The day of the Fall, despite all our repentance and remission, will remain the black hole into which the good of the world is eternally lost.

We may endeavor to love, thereafter, as ardently as we can, yet we will not recreate the lost purity, nor regain the most beautiful part of love which was annihilated. Our love could have been *so much greater*.

What we yet possess to offer at the hour of the highest Love will carry, whatever we do, this terrible mark.

This is why having profaned His gift of self makes the heart which yearns for the Absolute suffer until the end of life.

We would like to be God ourselves, to take back this day or these times, to give them the freshness of dawn and to guard them fearfully until the night.

From the first misstep, we know that we will no longer love as much as we could have. That is what makes repentance—because it cannot repair a broken man—so heartbreaking.

When we have known this pain of the irreparable, we seek beyond the possibilities of our heart, so that a few moments of sublime love, seized upon with great effort, can compensate for what fell in the swamps and in the shadows.

Part Four:

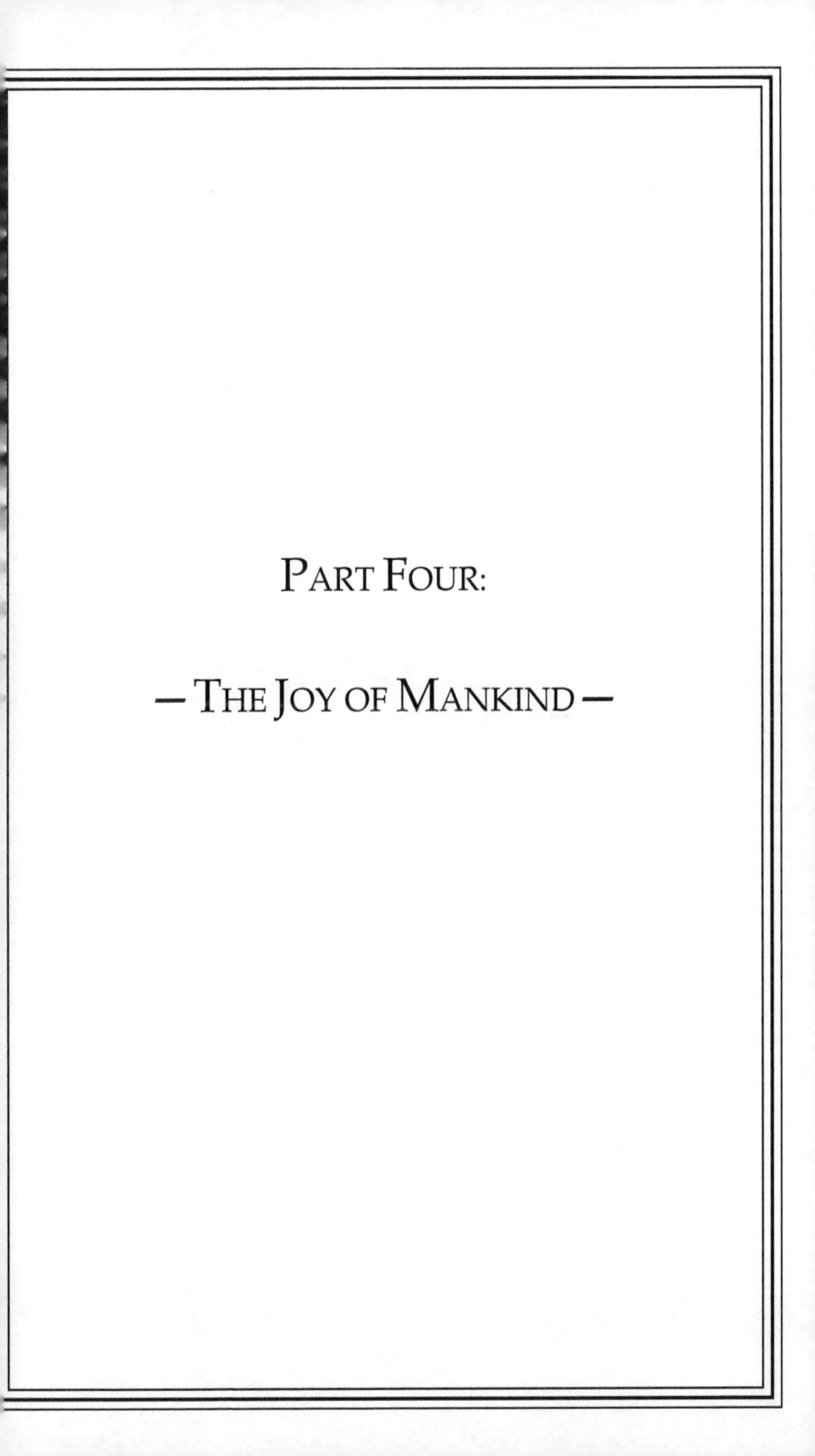

— The Joy of Mankind —

XV – Strong and Hard

The sun is gone. In half an hour it will be shade.

The birds, who sing madly in the gardens, perceive it.

There are roses everywhere, so gorged with light that they will soon perish.

The wood is already sleeping around a few tiled roofs.

As always, the birds now begin to utter their sharp cries and their pleas, no doubt for the two lovers sitting there, dreamy, with a huge white hat lying across their knees.

All of life seems condensed here; nothing lives apart from these birds, this dog which barks at the end of the world and these two hearts which steadily beat in the evening calm, heavy with the vibration of June.

How can one believe in hatred? Has one never seen the last roses go dim in the light evening silence?

We will have to tear ourselves away from this great country oasis soon.

It will be necessary to take, again, at the end of the path, the road where the cars tear up the ground through a sputtering, relentless rain.

There will be brutal lights, empty faces, soulless eyes.

This evening landscape is so clear, it is given with such a complete generosity! These dying roses, these bouquets of trees, these oat-fields shimmering and gray, these grave fir trees, all so pure and so simple that a childlike wonder rises in our beings, near this eternal youth of grasses, trees, and flowers.

We cannot hear anything anymore.

The night slicks down the roses.

The woods cut their jagged silhouette in the dying gleams. The last singing bird stops as if he too, from time to time, must simply listen to the silence. The two lovers have disappeared, hands trembling, a light wind in their hair.

I should move on.

I will go slowly, without disturbing the branches and the variety of life which slides through the shadows. I will guess the outline of things. I will feel the dew blooming at the end of the grass, which will refresh the sun tomorrow when it climbs over the top of the wood.

Where is the night of hearts, from which the tender morning would spring?

We will have to renew our sorrows, resume our journeys through the fields and lost woods, among cold hearts.

Who will understand later, in the savage glimmers, before our trembling eyes, that we have just left the forests and the wheat-fields, the shade and the silence?

But why falter? At the end of the path, we watch as cruel life snatches everything up in wolves' teeth.

We no longer look at anything, we no longer think, we

no longer breathe this air charged with the scent of passing death.

Put out the lights. Let the night weigh upon our hearts.

Tomorrow, when daybreak reaches the crest of the trees, we will have before us only the closed horizon of man.

We will have to be strong and hard, joyful through nothing but the radiance of our souls.

Dying evening, silent and sure of dawn, give us the peace of awaiting the light that is reborn, renewed, from the immense and auspicious night.

XVI – The Price of Life

We must reiterate the price of life. Life is the admirable instrument put in our hands, with which we forge our wills, raise our consciences, and build a monument of reason and of heart.

Life is not a form of sadness, but joy made flesh.

Joy of being useful.

Joy of mastering what could demean or weaken us.

Joy of acting and giving.

Joy of loving all that trembles, spirit and matter, because everything, under the impetus of a righteous life rises, lightens instead of weighing down.

You have to love life.

Sometimes, in times of weariness and disgust, we nearly lose our love of life.

You have to pull yourself together, straighten up.

Too many men are debased. But, alongside and in opposition to those whose baseness is a blasphemy to life, there are all those we see, or don't see, who redeem the world and bring honor to all life.

XVII – Despoliation

Happiness born of ignorance is not flattering.

It is a kind of narrow, vegetative happiness.

Intelligence has nothing to do with it, and neither does the body.

True happiness, happiness worthy of man, that which raises him up, is the happiness assured by the spirit,

Happiness born from the stripping of the soul, from the renunciation of the soul, in contemplation of human pleasures, is always made or broken by circumstances.

Happy is he who is not a slave to circumstances, he who knows how to enjoy pleasure as well as privation.

As long as one suffers from such a deprivation, as long as one suffers by comparing his material fate to others, we are neither happy nor free.

To remain in good spirits, even to live with one's soul apart from the world when the exterior universe holds nothing but a yawning void, to live intensely in this "material absence," to live without regret, master of your desires, having bent them to the complete domination of the spirit marks the victory of man, the true, the only victory, next to which the greatest conquests and dominions are merely caricatures of power.

Any comparison seems laughable next to the liberation brought by the mastery of the spirit over our possessions, our needs, and our chains.

We are freed from the old rusty chains that riveted us to mediocre conformities.

We hold Destiny in our hands, Destiny clearly discovered in its liberating nudity.

Happiness can be born everywhere. It comes, not from without, but from within us, holding within it infinite possibility.

XVIII – The Power of Joy

There are so many things that can bring you joy!

Even when, through our strength, we are free of our desires, we are happy.

Just the joy of living is itself so powerful!

Joy of having a radiant heart!

The joy of having a sturdy heart, arms and legs hard as trees, lungs that draw life and air!

Joy of having eyes that take on colors and shapes in their soft curves!

Joy of thinking, of spending hours drawing out the straight lines of reason or feasting on dreams!

Joy of believing, joy of loving, of giving oneself, of striding through life, flexible as water!

How can one be unhappy!

It is so simple, so basic, so natural!

Through the worst calamities, happiness always bursts forth like a geyser which we try to obstruct in vain.

Happiness and life are the same thing.

To be no longer happy is to doubt one's body, the warmth of one's blood, the consuming fire of one's heart, to doubt these great lights of the spirit which bathe all of existence.

Even misfortune still brings us the joys of the soul which gives of its own blood, which weighs out its sacrifice, which feels deeply misfortune's bitter sting.

A cruel joy, but a higher joy, a joy reserved for the man whose broken heart understands.

XIX – To Dream, to Think

The hours of dreams are hours of profound life, where all the poetry that floats in our consciousness gets up and runs in wisps.

Then the sun comes.

The snowy fog descends as if called down by the river. We see before us the bright, clear sword of water. And reason reorders and assembles the scattered discoveries sprung from the dream, unifying them under its dominion.

Joy to find, to compare! Joy of giving meaning and direction! Joy of understanding and of scaling the slopes and the summits of the true, the beautiful and the useful!

The mind orders it into clear, parallel lines and extracts the laws revealed within. Man feels then that he is master of all the elements, master of this disproportionate universe where his brain, no bigger than a bird or a fallen fruit, imposes a comprehensive order and harmony.

Whoever does not know how to enjoy the possibilities of dreaming and thinking, offered to man every second, ignores the nobility of life.

We can always be enchanted, for dreams are our secret cellos.

One can always think, that is to say, having the mind not only occupied, but vibrant, tending towards a domination more powerful, more exhilarating than the fire of a thousand desires.

To be bored is to give up the dream and the spirit.

Boredom is the disease of empty souls and brains. Life quickly becomes a horribly dull chore.

Love itself is exalted and amazed only to the extent that

the superior being nourishes poetry, strengthens the impulses of sensitivity.

One must still dream and ponder over their love.

XX – Patience

Patience is the first of victories, victory over oneself, over one's nerves, over one's weaknesses.

As long as we have not acquired it, life is only a cascade of capitulations, capitulations made in struggle, certainly, crying out in what we perceive to be manifestations of authority, but which are in fact only an abdication to petty pride.

To be patient is to wait for one's hour, finger on the trigger, as one watches for prey; it is to build each of the day's actions in consideration of order and balance, laying carefully the foundation stones that will support the building.

Patience delivers the joy of not having given in.

Impatience leaves the heart with the reproach of having been exiled and of having been the author of vanity and vain agitation.

XXI – Obedience

No great work is accomplished in selfishness and pride.

Obeying is a joy because it is a form of gift, of clairvoyant gift.

Obeying is fruitful, multiplying the result of efforts tenfold.

Obeying is a duty, because the common good depends on the disciplined coming-together of many energies.

Human society is not formed by a cloud of fierce and fanciful mosquitoes, rushing in the wind according to their personal interest and their mood. It is a large, sensitive complex, made sterile or dangerous by anarchy, to which order and harmony give unlimited possibilities.

A rich people of millions in population, but selfishly isolated and atomized, is a dead people.

A poor people where everyone intelligently recognizes their limits and their communal obligations, obeys and works as a team, is a people with life. Obedience is the highest form of the use of freedom.

It is a constant manifestation of authority, authority over oneself, the most difficult of all.

No one is really capable of commanding others who is not first able to command himself, to tame in him the proud wanderer who would have liked to throw himself madly into the winds of adventure.

After having obeyed, one may command, not as a brute, enjoying the right to crush others, but because command is a magnificent prerogative when it aims to discipline unruly forces, to lead them to the fullness of obedience, to this superior source of joy.

XXII – Kindness

Sometimes a word, a single word, an affectionate gesture, a look full of sincere friendship, can save a man on the brink of the abyss.

By affection and by example we can do anything.

Shouting and storming about rarely solve problems.

You have to be good-hearted, discover what is going on among the fog of each heart, temper the necessary reproach with a friendly joke that gives hope, always put yourself in the shoes of the other, in the soul of the other, think of your personal reaction if you had received the observation, the encouragement, the reprimand, instead of addressing it to others.

Most of the men are grown-ups, quite vicious but still sensitive, tense towards affection.

There are not thirty-six routes to guide them, there is only one: that of the heart.

The other roads sometimes seem easier to take, but ultimately, they do not lead anywhere.

XXIII – Happy Isolation

The company of others is, most of the time, nothing but restlessness, noise, troubles revolving around mutual loneliness.

To constantly search for what is called *stimulation*, is to be afraid of being in the presence of yourself.

It is, in reality, to take flight morally.

How can you confuse joy with being constantly mixed-up in the tumultuous crowd?

Why should one absolutely have to be swallowed up among other beings to believe oneself happy?

One is then only in contact with the tree bark of others, one enjoys only their artificial or superficial attitudes.

This can obviously give distraction, temporary pleasure, a kind of breath of wind or fresh air.

But what a gulf between this shallow "pleasure" and the deep, essential joy of conversation with yourself, the analysis of one's own intimate thoughts and one's most secret sensitivity!

There we see everything; we go to the source of everything.

To deny the power, the magnitude of this true joy, is to deny the whole inner life.

Loneliness is a wonderful opportunity for the soul to get to know itself, to keep watch, to learn.

Only empty heads or fickle hearts are afraid of remaining silent in front of themselves.

It is at such times that we see if our feelings are solid or if they were nothing but noise.

High feelings can live alone, without physical presence;

on the contrary, isolation purifies and grows them.

The joy, the joy that spreads like a block of granite under the water of flowing life, the one that never gives up and which never disappoints, lies in the inner struggle, in the inner exaltation: to watch over oneself, to dominate oneself, to purify oneself, to rise, to have the courage to think.

Because it is so simple to be lazy or cowardly in the face of spiritual work!

Have the energy to expand your hidden world! To love intensely, that is to say, to give oneself silently, without reluctance!

We prefer to forget or deny that these fundamental joys exist, to be satisfied with immediate enjoyments that we believe to be superior to everything, and after which we have nothing, very often, if not dust in the heart and a wilting of the wings.

The mystics have long known this constant animation of the interior life.

Were they less happy, did they have less joy than we who chatter, mingled with faces where we only discover appearances, fed by words that die with the echo?

The joy of the mystics is just one example.

The same inner joy exists at other stages of spirituality and sensitivity.

The presence of others is not even essential at all.

One can perfectly love, be possessed by the highest joys

of the heart, in physical distance and even in death.

As long as we have not once freed ourselves from external elements, as long as we have not been able to live alone, that is to say in the most real company, that nothing can disturb, we have not yet reached the very threshold of joy.

Instead of complaining about loneliness, you have to bless it, you have to take advantage of this unexpected possibility of examining yourself in silence and dominating yourself lucidly, completely, even in your most contradictory thoughts.

Doors closed to the world? Willful termination of contact with the outside?

So much the better!

Because it means, if you like: doors open to the soul, exact contact with one's self; exhilarating joys of knowledge, spiritual fulfillment and, mystically, the most delicate and complete gift.

XXIV – Grandeur

It is often by doing, with maximum nobility, a thousand bothersome little things that you are great.

It is infinitely more difficult to stretch your soul a thousand times, every day, without relief, than to give a single grand impulse at the moment of a visionary event.

Merit to be given there is slight.

The magnitude of the fleeting opportunity alone gives us the strength to act, the desire to astonish, while allowing us to have the highest opinion of ourselves.

You can do a great thing wonderfully and be far from real greatness.

Greatness is the nobility of the soul wearing down, dripping with the desire to give, each according to our duties, especially when they are stripped of those things that give rise to vanity.

For both women and men.

Greatness for a woman is often to give herself hour by hour to dull, even prosaic housework.

Yet who will admire it?

Who will know the thousand battles fought, in the bottom of the heart, in laziness, in pride, in singing passions, in the softness which calls the soul and the body towards the warm sands of easy life?

The one who despite all this advances, resists, progresses, is great since the gift of herself was total, without requiring the vanity of recognition.

So many high-status people always complain, find everything unpleasant, never know how to rejoice frankly of nothing!

Everything seems boring to them because they never give themselves up, because they approach each moment, even when it would require only a small exertion, with the firm intention of delivering only the bare minimum, and even then with reluctance.

Everything is a question of giving freely.

Happy people are those who give themselves. The dissatisfied are those who strangle their existence with a perpetual retraction, constantly wondering what they will lose.

Virtue, greatness, happiness, everything revolves around that: give yourself! Give yourself completely, all the time. Do what you have to do, bravely, with maximum application, even if the object is merely housework, without apparent grandeur.

Wherever you are, above or below, man or woman, the problem is exactly the same: it is giving that differentiates clear souls from troubled souls.

Part Five:

— A Man's Duty —

(Notes from the Eastern Front)

XXV – The Great Retreat

To die twenty years too early or twenty years too late is of no consequence.

All that matters is to find a good death.

Only with this goal in mind can we truly begin to live.

As a simple soldier, I would gladly die tomorrow. The humility of my lot in life at the front reconciled me such an outcome. Not having lived as a saint, to die as a soldier's soul would be the most suitable thing.

Are my weeks numbered? Then it is best to make the most of these chances to purify our souls. I once dreamed of dying after a long illness, to better prepare myself for the inevitable. But such a death necessarily takes place in an atmosphere of pollution.

On the front, our preparation takes place in a feeling of power, in the unfolding of the will. I realize how lucky I am.

Perhaps I will return alive, more alive than ever before?

Either way, this great retreat, which life or death will close, will have been a blessing. I enjoy it freely, fully, like a nourishing and beautiful sun.

Why should I tremble under its fire?

The soldier learns to be great among the most mundane or the most painful things. Heroism is to stand, to struggle, to be always alert, happy and strong, in nameless, unrecognized misery of the front, in the mud, the excrement, the corpses, the mist of water and snow, the endless and colorless fields, the total absence of outer joy.

Every day we move further away from the blissful world of yesteryear. Are we not already half-dead, we who advance, gritting our teeth, through the mists?

Always look at those who have less than you and rejoice in what you have, never lusting after ephemeral desires.

Life is always beautiful when you look at it with peaceful eyes, the light of a soul at peace.

We soldiers, we have nothing, and we are happy.

The joy of an unencumbered soul can only flourish when one has cast off this jumble of mental slavery.

War is not just combat. Above all, it is a long, sometimes exhausting streak, sometimes stretching into tedium, of silent renouncements, of daily sacrifices, without relief.

Virtue is forged in the same way everywhere.

The privations, endured with humility, waiting patiently for Death's arrival, the giving of one's self — far from the spotlight, one plays one's part in unknown fields and groves, in this wasteland far from all human joy.

Such is the real war, the one waged by millions of men who will never know ostentatious glory and who — if they do not die — will return home with their faces tight, their lips closed, for others would not comprehend the heartbreaks and renunciations in their obscure heroism.

The crowd is only struck by heroism when it is bright and loud. What impresses the public is brilliance, not the painful and slow ascent of souls who rise in silence and shadow to greatness.

But are we ever understood? Do we hear, do we see anything other than the superficial? The bottom of hearts is such an abyss of desires, denials, sorrows that we prefer not to approach it. It is simpler, more pleasant to stick to the superficial and, without thinking too much, to enjoy the words and attitudes that weave the tapestry of human drama.

We, we soldiers, stand behind that tapestry. What souls will imagine our journeys; who will have the strength to join us spiritually?

Zeal, even intelligence, cannot be enough.

To have culture is to have a balance of mind, illumination, wisdom, which can only be the result of a long discipline of the higher faculties, where the only proven method is the application of extensive contact with the most fundamental works of human intelligence.

The disinterested study of ancient civilizations, fathers of ideas and systems, the study of Philosophy, the study of Mathematics, the secret fabric of all the Arts, the comparative study of the lessons of history, this alone can bring about the harmony of the human faculties, without which the most dazzling successes always have a character of miracle and fragility.

Intellectual maturity is not irreconcilable with genius.

Maturity makes genius exact and human, channeling it towards a desirable end. Its strength is not thereby diminished, only more useful. Richelieu would not have given France half of the blessings of his genius if he had been self-taught.

The origin of our century's mental debilitation is that it is the century of the self-taught. Their work has a disorderly, inhuman, unstable character. True genius, or at least beneficent genius, is balanced, which brings happiness, progress, and order.

The instinctive genius is stunning, dazzling, but always at a great cost.

When the fireworks fade, the sky only looks darker than before.

The banal and the vulgar are neighbors of the grandiose and the eternal.

Earlier I watched a pig going to slaughter. He was keen on life, poor thing. Almost bloodless, still he gasped and moaned. Beasts and men, in the face of death, we are the same. Yet, our honor demands, and we must take great care to ensure, that at the hour of our death we have the courage to face it with dignity.

Soldiers, we risk our own skins all the time, and so we take very simple joy in merely existing.

Death is always right before our face. Death is everywhere. Therefore, we understand the greatness of life better than others.

Part Five: A Man's Duty

If the soul did not rise, straight as the barrel of a gun, straight as the crosses over the graves, we would quickly sink into moral decay.

Our whole world consists of woods, fields, marshes, stripped trees, near which one is on the lookout, day or night, warming his hands with his breath, rubbing his ears, trampling over ground that is today as hard and unforgiving as granite where just yesterday it was a sea of mud.

In the evening, from four o'clock, we watch the shadows. We must guard our hearts closely so as not to weep in the face of such an abyss. The soul is faced with total surrender.

And yet, she is proud and she sings, because, stripped bare as in the bygone days of innocence, she is aware of the gravity of the mission offered to those who tread this lonely abyss, those who will redeem the cowardice and filth of a world peopled by empty souls.

Here her wings start to beat again, shaking off the dried mud that once had dirtied them. They find joy again in the return to clean air, open space, distant lines.

If we, here, have made good of our suffering, we will have achieved our true victory.

But will we who suffer be able to remain pure to the end?

Won't we feel ridiculous, in our angelic garb, on our return?

Will we have the courage not to be ashamed when we hear the countless jeers of those who have soiled their souls, and who insolently believe themselves to be triumphant?

XXVI – The Taming of Horses

Fleas cling to our uniforms in serried ranks. Mice run all about. In the middle of the night, I awake to find a rat nestled against my nose.

These companions strengthen us against vanity and pride, we who cannot escape even the smallest of beasts, the most ridiculous and the dirtiest.

But poetry is everywhere. In front of our guns, thousands of sparrows jump in the hedges, round-bellied birds slowly dancing about. They listen, a meter away, to the little compliments that we offer them. Then they settle in wild flocks in the rushes; they cry, chirp, and hiss, as if the silver sky had thrown fistfuls of pure joy over the frosty landscape. There are also passing ravens, like black lightning, few and silent: from time to time they utter their great hoarse cry, no doubt to remind us that death awaits us, harsh like them, ravenous like them, on dark and deadly wings.

We strive to always smile, at the singing sparrows, at the solemn crows that pass.

But the heart is the heart; and every man, though smiling with his mouth and eyes, hides underneath the awful secrets of a suffering animal.

Part Five: A Man's Duty

We feel that death watches on every side. Each step exacts a cost. Our steps grow heavy and must be made light, despite the heavy guns, the stumbling feet, the fields of overripe grain that scratch the skin, the massive shell-holes into which a misplaced step could drop one into the abyss without a word.

This is it, the thankless life of a soldier, which knows neither exhilaration nor glory, where, at any time, one can be stabbed, shot, or dragged off as a prisoner by the enemy on the other side. You have to move forward calmly, meter by meter, even when shots may ring out suddenly from ten paces away. Shots ring out in the night, between the outposts, a hoarse cry, and the night rolls on, impervious, frozen, relentless. At these times our entire being wishes to rebel. We care for our lives, those of our comrades, the blood coursing powerfully through their veins; we are beings of the flesh; we want the light to be reborn. With vigor and heat, the human beast roars and cries out for his will to unfold, to burn, to resound.

To remain huddled, subdued, to remain in the shadows, ready for the final act or the final breath, takes a terrible discipline. It inflicts terrible injuries on our will.

But our taste for life will be even stronger, because we have more intensely experienced the value, the flavor, the burning sweetness of each second, falling like a drop of silence in this great tension of ready hearts.

We love, with unchained power, our carnal existence, the rhythm of our thoughts, the momentum of our senses, which a single bullet in the night could shatter.

Our arms! Our legs! Our eyes! To surround, to cross, to regard with passion and domination!

All this screams man's right to life, the right of the animal that wants to run and seize, the right of the intelligence that wants to enchant and create.

Life! How beautiful, indescribably beautiful, exhilarating, softness of body, light of midday, ardor of fire!

We clench this life in our willful fists, those of silent, attentive, patient shadow-watchers.

We have learned to tame ourselves, to tame the wild horses which ran across the vast fields of our dreams.

But holding them in our hands with a steel fist, we close our eyes and inhale the powerful smell of life that gathers above. Life! Life!

It is so cold that the medicine vials shattered. The alcohol itself froze in the ambulance. Poor feet, poor ears, poor frostbitten noses, mummified in the atrocious, howling, whistling night…

This morning the order to leave for another combat sector arrived.

We will go where we are ordered, smiling in the snow which, since we awoke, has been falling in heavy flakes.

Our feet will be cold, our lips will be raw, our bodies, huddled over against the cold, will be heavy and awkward, but our inner fire will continue to rise and fill our eyes with glimmers of the sun.

Here our souls are strained. These low hills, these rows of firs, these abandoned millstones watch us go, regarding our lines with shining eyes.

This black sky that I contemplate now for the last time, I have filled it with the brilliant streaks of tracer bullets while the enemy's rounds uttered their shrill cries, like pouncing cats, all about me.

Already my bag is packed. I look at the crushed straw, broken into smaller pieces on the spot I habitually rested after returning, tired and frozen, from late night patrols. The smoky little lantern casts a yellow light over my last daily report. A few more shirts, a few handkerchiefs, freshly washed, already covered with dust. Rough mud walls, the oven that we heated with debris from barricades, little frozen tiles, painted with designs of white ferns...

We pick up our battered bowls, our canteens, our weapons emblazoned with black lightning.

No doubt, to this place will one day return plants laden with fruit, Christian icons, a woman clad in heavy petticoats, and the thick smell of vegetable fat. But forever gone will be the humble and bustling life of many young foreign boys, lost in the depths of the steppe, who left in the middle of the night with calloused hands and frozen blood.

This miserable, poorly-lit square has been the center of an intense spiritual life. That life will leave with us and will be reborn at random from the frozen roads, improvised lodgings, embankments, and trenches from which we watch for and track down our opponent, or avoid his blows.

We may return to these spots one day: but the essential character will be gone.

And so, we leave at dawn without looking back. Life is ahead, even if life is death.

Bah! the greater the sacrifice, the more we give of ourselves.

And it was to give of ourselves that we stood up, with radiant hearts.

XXVII – The Apocalyptic Cycle

The wind blows in biting gusts, whipping the snow against our skin like darts. The river is frozen; frozen, its little tributaries which ran through the crevasses; frozen, the hills, the thistles of the embankments, the ruined factories.

My heart itself has caught cold, cold from these months of soul-tension, of withdrawal into inhuman solitude; cold as these rigid black trees which the north wind whips.

Distress in everything...

Everyone feels the chill. We break our cold bread. We scrape the huge chunks of mud from our clothes with a knife. We cut away great clumps of the blackish glue from our shoes and gaiters.

No water. You have to go three kilometers to procure a dirty brown liquid filled with grass clippings.

Let us love our misery anyway, as it uplifts us, prepares

us for destinies that call for pure and strong hearts.

The cycle of wars is now apocalyptic: the waves widen more and more, grow in speed and force, to spread in a fabulous gyrating movement.

Wars have become universal revolutions.

The whole world is caught up in its whirlwind: armies collide, economic forces clash, they tear each other apart, the forces of the spirit engage in a merciless duel.

The universe will have to bleed, struggle, know the pangs of flight, the agony of separation. Thousands of men, millions of men will have to look with frozen or feverish eyes at Death, always the same, that is to say always cruel, tearing the heart at the same time as the flesh. This drama was inevitable. Only the blind and the foolish, that is to say almost everyone, believed that these were conflicts of rival nations, conflicts which could be localized.

However, these are implacable pseudo-religious wars, quite similar to all religious wars, but which will take almost limitless proportions, reaching up to the last little island or ice floe, so that all people, be they Tahitians or Laplanders, will have to choose like everyone else.

When, how, will this prodigious settling of accounts end?

Our skies will long be crossed by this lightning. Our children will grow up amid the blinding flashes of falling or triumphing ideas-at-arms.

A century where the scale of the drama chills the

blood—but a sorrowful century in which the whole universe is being remade, more by spirit than by iron.

Tragedy such as the world has never known so complete, in which we are all actors, but where it is hearts that play. Millions of hearts are on the scene, still young and naive, or old and silent, or ruined, or confused.

To walk a hundred meters between the muddy lines, we come back broken, as if every step took all our strength.

Nothing to do.

Nothing to read. We only have a miserable kerosene lamp, with a small yellowish flame that lights up a square meter of our shelter.

It takes more courage to live like this holed up in the mud than to advance on the enemy with the machine gun under your arm. You can feel the temptation, the muffled voices, the demoralizing questions: "What are you doing here? Can't you see you're wasting your time? Your efforts? Your sacrifices? Does anyone even remember that you exist? Shall we leave you alone to rot away into oblivion...?"

But the soul quickly regains its serenity; she knows that nothing is more precious than this renunciation, this silent descent into the depths of consciousness. Can the real victory, the victory over oneself, be better acquired elsewhere than in the midst of these humiliations, welcomed with the head held high, by straightforwardly opposing this hostile environment, the loneliness of the heart, and the cunning of the enemy which assault the spirit?

XXVIII – Enlightenment

War, for us soldiers, is to be among poor companions with grim faces, men huddled under the frozen earth, defined by dark suffering, without comfort; it is mud, it is the snow, it is bottomless despair, it is feet torn by the endless steps, it's the hundred shameful little miseries which surround the life of the soldier at the front, like a clinging and fog of sadness.

This stifled life ceaselessly calls for the calling up of energy, the leap of the soul, which must tear itself out of that mist in order to shine again.

This life bears no resemblance to the brilliant ideas that the public has about the exploits of war. But they ought not be disabused of this notion. We would thereby spoil their beautiful and brightly-colored image.

Yet I lie down in exhaustion at the end of each day with a joy that is a little bit sad, but powerful, because it is an incomparable lesson in patience, self-mortification, the elevation of the soul.

We should never try to cheat the ordeal or stifle its voice. If the lesson were to be useless, if we did not return as men changed by the experience, there would not be this wall between, on one hand, those who were afraid of the ordeal, and on the other, those who looked hardship in the eye and learned from it.

Life sinks its fangs into us time after time. I escaped this time, like so many others, with a weary, worried, chewed-up heart. I wish now to return there at peace, having found innocence in confidence.

It is Christmas. I watch the snow falling tirelessly, and, despite its lightness, I feel that I am suffocating.

Soldiers pass, bent double against the wind, going quickly.

Around me, nothing; always the wind blowing, a man nervously biting his nails, others collapsing into sleep, exhausted by the nights on the watch.

Jesus could have been born in our little shelter.

Sincerity of the good animals about the manger, who offered themselves entirely...

The honest hearts of the shepherds, who did not doubt for a second, did not hesitate, and who immediately gave everything at their disposal...

They only had sheep, and they gave their sheep.

Who, remembering them, would not take heart? What counts is not what you give, sheep or great treasures: it is the fervor of the heart that weighs upon the scales.

Sometimes life seems too exhausting to carry, painful even to think about.

Today it is almost an anguish.

To forget your own existence, your screaming soul!

What could let us forget?

We have spent the day killing by the dozens the lice that

chew at our skin. That is all. And yet the soul must stand tall, proud, steadfast.

And it must stay that way.

But great muffled voices, deep in the background, moan.

We are not men differently built than the others. We too would like, when we listen only to the calls of that outer life, to do naught but pile up money earned without labor. All men desire this, whose bodies run hot, whose eyes are alight with that mixture of desire and pleasure. The human beast, youth, the need to dominate, rears up in distress: are you not wasting your years of radiant life? Watched by death every hour, don't you have any regrets, feel the desire to break everything and run, to throw yourself towards pleasure, towards luminous faces, towards beautiful women as the other boys of your time?...

These are times when you have to stifle your passions to feed your soul and your faith, at the expense of such human desires that shine before our eyes like a mirage.

We stand guard on our icy parapets, with a touch of bitterness in our hearts, but supremely happy yet at the sacrifice renewed every day, without even knowing if we will ever be understood.

End of the year. I recap the line of dying days.

This year with its secrets and its illuminating lights...

The secrets that are hidden behind a smile, but which often bleed, like wounds never closed...

And then, the lights, lights shown upon our character and our deeds.

There are the lights that we may show others. They are the least beautiful. These heroic lights we show to others, they maintain an air of theatricality and falseness, even when displayed in modest fashion. It is only with great difficulty that one can keep a truly naïve heart, and yet also take care to avoid an excess of pride...

These lights, these imperfect lights will remain superficial. But these glorious lights hurt our eyes. We are blinded when we leave them. And we are so often plunged from these bright lights into the shadows of everyday banality or minor setbacks!

I remember those lights. I love them only to the extent that they illuminated that ideal towards which I walk.

I should only like these lights for this reason. But I know very well that I have often let myself be taken in by my own self-satisfaction. Finally, these lights, necessary to rouse us to action, sadden me because they show me that, over and over again, I find myself biting down on the hook of vanity or pride.

And then there are the other lights, the ones that no one else sees from the outside. They light up our souls like X-rays. Then you know exactly what you are worth. Caught by these lights, we are no longer very proud. We see clearly all of our weaknesses, we see clearly the poverty of the excuses we have made for a hundred mistakes, always the same.

But it is precisely because we know our own mediocrity all too well that we experience intoxicating joys when the lights that emerge from the depths of the soul end up illuminating a heroic work of our own doing. Though it be only a small act, it was born after so much secret cowardice that that first inner smile plunges us into unspeakable raptures.

XXIX – Intransigence

Who kept us on their thoughts, the lost boys of the steppes, who had nothing to drink to the new year but melted snow, streaked with bits of yellow grass, or a few sips of artificial coffee that smelled of soap?

Miserable details, humiliating details, the evocation of which seems out of place: who else could imagine how the biting cold made a herculean effort of even minor tasks, for example the miserable, inevitable sickness of dysentery?

Of course, we had no sewers. Fifteen, twenty times, in just a few hours, you would have to run into the blizzard to relieve yourself, allowing your body to be cut by a wind as sharp as a blade, as sharp as a whip.

Vanity of our bodies, in which we often took such pride!

The beautiful human beast, strong, burning with life, must submit to these humiliations! The body rebels, but must give in.

The body that was so satisfied with the pleasant rhythms of life! Body which has been caressed, kissed, loved: and we heap such shame upon you!

Yet nothing can reach the mind that is master over itself. If the body is humiliated, it is because the will has led him into these whistling snows, to the bottom of these sordid shelters. Yesterday it was lice. Today the cold claws at our skin. We willed it to be so. We do not care that we are scourged by this hostile, ferocious situation. One day, the cruel winds will die off with the return of the leaves to the trees. Our bodies, stretched out in the waters of the rivers, in the sun and in the winds, will feel life beating more ardently than ever around their bones, strong as metal, under living flesh like the flesh of flowers, hard and clean like marble, but golden, full, vibrant! Having suffered and triumphed, we will open our arms to the sun.

And our smooth, powerful, and rough bodies will flow with blood like the sap of the great virgin trees!

Our wills will bring back to life the beautiful human beast, prancing with life, now tamed.

The whole steppe, caught up in the turmoil, might well crackle, whistle, rise in gigantic waves.

Despite the cold that scorched us, despite the gusts of hailstones that riddled our faces, I faced the maelstrom a hundred times, to fill my eyes with this grandeur. I felt carried away by the squalls, I communicated with this epic power where the white plain, the sky, and the wind mingled their strength, their leaps, their icy flames, their long cries springing from the horizon and howling away at the end of the quivering plain.

What are, at such moments, the forces which rise up in us, in communion with the great natural outbursts? I then feel transported, an immense bliss rises from all my body, as if fabulous correspondences were established between my blood which runs and the wind which blows, between the life which boils in my limbs and the savage life which blows past under the great sky.

There is not one of us soldiers who does not have to be prepared for the most gruesome endings.

But do we give only with reservation?

Death in humiliation, isn't it a way of giving even more?

True sacrifice cannot be calculated, cannot be given with reservation.

We listen to cynics more readily than to the message of righteous hearts. Yet pure hearts will have victory. Only idealists will change the world.

I am writing near a rusty barrel, at the bottom of which floats the last bits of steppe grass suspended in our icy water. This poverty, this isolation, we know them because we desired sincerity. And, more than ever, in this solitude where bodies and hearts feel invaded by mortal cold, I renew my oaths of intransigence.

More than ever, I will go straight ahead, without giving in, without rest, hard on my soul, hard on my desires, hard on my youth.

I'd rather see ten years of cold and abandonment, than one day feeling my soul emptied, voided of its living dreams.

I write these words without trembling, which nevertheless make me suffer. In the hour of a world's bankruptcy, souls are needed which may stand hard and tall as rocky cliffs, beaten in vain by raging waves.

XXX – The Cross

Which moment will be our end?

Death passes unresponsive and his hands strangle hearts at random. The machine-gun fires, it whizzes, it cracks, or it pierces with its deadly fingers a young man's body.

What to do, if not to have a pure heart, a quiet regard to the timely sacrifice, made freely? If it comes, our eyelashes will not quiver, and we will leave with the faint, sad smile of the tender memories that surround our last seconds.

If we come back, even though the warmth of life will have made us forget this icy breath, our hearts will forever have the composure of a life that has not trembled before death.

May fate always find us strong and worthy!

You still have to love happiness, as you love the song of the wind, however fleeting it may be, as you love the colors of the evening, even though you know they are going to die.

For the great winds are reborn and sing again and, every day, the colors return to the blazing axis of the risen sun.

It is not up to us to keep the winds from dying, or to prevent the sun from fading, but to draw strength from them while they yet live.

Joy is the fire of indomitable hearts, and no reversal can extinguish or stifle its burning colors.

When you see the waves retreating from the sands, returning to the dark depths of the sea, think of the great outpouring that will return a few hours later, white, shimmering in the sun, bold and strong, as if these waves were the vanguard of an assault on the world itself!

To be happy is to be unselfish.

Happiness is just that: giving all of oneself.

There are so many mediocre things on earth, low or ugly, that one day we would be overwhelmed by them if we did not carry within ourselves the fire which burns away ugliness, which consumes it and purifies us.

Art is our inner salvation, our secret garden that constantly refreshes and soothes us. Poetry, painting, sculpture, music, anything but to escape from the mundane, to rise above the drying dust, to create something grand, instead of submitting to the small, to let out that spark of the extraordinary that each of us possesses, and convert it into a grandiose, devouring, inextinguishable fire.

The dead and dark centuries are those where souls hesitated before this effort. The luminous centuries are those which have seen these great fires of souls mark out, dominate, the mountains of the spirit.

The only true joys are not those that others give us, but those that we carry within us, that our faith creates, that fill us with dynamism.

The rest comes like the foam of the sea, shining at the tip of the waves, quivering for a moment on the edge of the sands, then quickly dies, or withdraws with the waves.

This is the happiness that others bring us from time to time.

The joy that arises from our passion for life and our will is like the great force which rumbles and rolls at the bottom of the sea, which springs up to meet the sun and is renewed every second.

As if hanging from a boat, we watch the mighty sea throw its waves like immense leopard skins, spread out, supple and shiny, standing up like a silver flame or like a prodigious spray of white flowers! This life constantly returns, rebounds; we know that nothing, until the end of the world, will stop this momentum!

So must be our hearts, brash, but like this wonderful rhythmic force: ordered, chanted like an eternal song.

During the day, we are caught up in poor, often trivial concerns.

But at night, the imagination weaves itself through our dreams, takes us in its fantasies, its reconstruction or anticipation.

Sometimes I am amazed by the relentless lucidity of dreams.

Of course, the dream is often a wild folly, a phantasm. But it is often also for me a meeting with my conscience and with my first intuitions.

I see myself naturally, as I am when my will is not there to lock its brakes upon the movement of my passions.

I then know exactly on which points I doubt myself.

Each time I must say to myself: look, here you falter.

I thus have the almost daily proof that I can resist a thousand temptations, lead my life with honor only to the extent that a renewed effort masters and restrains, every day, deep within myself, a wild horse, which can never be fully tamed, and which only the whip of the will, wielded unceasingly, can contain.

If the watch were relaxed, everything would come undone.

I see this in my dreams.

Will the will itself fall asleep? I awake, defeated, the dream has cut me adrift.

There is no more decisive examination of conscience for me than the unfolding of dreams. Dreams lay bare my soul before me, leaves deep marks upon my thoughts, with the knowledge that we must always be on guard over our baser impulses, because these baser elements do not naturally run towards but, on the contrary, run from it as soon as they are tempted by beautiful falsehoods.

The soul, freed by the gift it has made of itself, flies,

soars and sings.

Because we hear within us these great songs of serenity, we know that the work we embark upon will be beautiful. For the great and the beautiful can only be created in joy and in faith.

If we love virtue only in so far as it is taken notice of, we defile it with pride. We are no longer virtuous the moment we desire the virtue, which we believe we have achieved, to be seen and admired.

So it is with all virtues. They are beautiful, soft, radiant, if we love them for themselves, if we cultivate them for the unique pleasure of having reached them.

We come to life without thinking or caring that we might not be understood by others.

Uncomplicated hearts cannot imagine the complications of others. Fresh hearts cannot imagine other hearts being hateful or defiled.

Suffering is the most wonderful of companions, pathetic and angelic, washing souls of all desire, raising them to the heights they had dreamed of for so long.

Defeats, victories, dreams or material successes pass away, are forgotten, fires that shine for a moment, scents swept away by a passing wind.

But the essential, the unique, is for us the great spiritual conflagration without which the world is nothing.

So long as there remains a little fire in some corner of the world, all miracles of greatness remain possible.

Everything in life is a matter of faith and tenacity. Trust cannot be begged for, it has to be won. And the best way to conquer is to first give of yourself.

We all carry our cross: we must carry it with a proud smile, so that we know that we are stronger than suffering and also so that those who seek to harm us understand that their arrows reach us in vain.

What does it matter if you suffer if you have had a few immortal hours in your life?

At least we have lived!

Part Six:

— To Give Completely —

XXXI – The Reconquest

The turmoil that agitates public opinion, the wars that shake up nations, are just episodes.

Partial reforms will do away with such periodic chaos.

To attempt to change people would be a very disappointing work if it were not accompanied by the essential work of changing that which lies deep in the soul, by a transformation of the very foundations of our time.

All the scandals, the decline of honesty and honor, shamelessness in the certainty of impunity, the passion for money which sweeps away conventions, dignity, self-respect, amorality, which has become unconscious, indicate the existence of a deep-seated evil which calls for remedies of equal magnitude. It is not suddenly that we lie, that we break all moral laws, supernatural or natural, and, more simply, the laws of the public code. It is not overnight that you work yourself up to bold hypocrisy, to speak truth only with reticence, to lie with virtuous words.

This deformation of consciousness which amazes, which frightens, today, or which puts on an air of sarcastic superiority, is only the conclusion of a long decline in human virtues.

It is the passion for wealth, the will to be powerful no matter what, it is the frenzy to be honored, it is materialism, it is the unscrupulous gratification of instincts, which have corrupted men and, through men, institutions.

The world is more and more preoccupied with banal, material, or simply animal joys. It maintains itself only by the principle of maximizing material wealth. Each man lives only for himself and allows the domination of life both within his own home and within the country by a constant egoism which has converted men into hateful, embittered, greedy wolves, or corrupt and soulless half-men.

We will come out of this downfall only through an immense moral recovery, by re-teaching men to love, to sacrifice themselves, to live, to struggle and to die for a higher ideal.

In a century when we live only for ourselves, it will take hundreds, thousands of men to live no longer for themselves, but for a collective ideal, accepting in advance all the sacrifices, all the humiliations, all necessary heroism.

All that matters is faith, brilliant confidence, the complete absence of selfishness and individualism, the pulling of the whole being towards service, without promise of reward, in any place, by any means, towards a cause that goes beyond man, asking him everything, promising him nothing.

The only things that count are the quality of the soul, the pulse, the total gift, the will to hoist an ideal above all else, in the most absolute selflessness.

The time is coming when saving the world will require this handful of heroes and saints to make the great Reconquest.

Part Six: To Give Completely

XXXII – Flotilla of Souls

Nations recover rapidly from financial setbacks.

They may reconstitute without too much difficulty a new political framework.

All that is needed is skilled technicians and a willingness to work together.

Great revolutions are not political or economic. These are small revolutions, changes of purely mechanical nature. When the specialists put the pieces together, when the engines have found their rhythm and stern-faced foremen have been set to watch over them, the material revolution is accomplished.

The rest will only require repairs from time to time, a modification here and there. The machine is fitted or overhauled. The gears turn. Most of the work is done.

The real revolution is far more complicated, one which brings together not the machinery of the state but the secret life of every soul.

There, it is no longer a matter of automatic review and monitoring. It is about the vices and the virtues, the impulses towards profundity and weaknesses, the desperate hopes that are so dear to us...

What is there at the bottom of that gaze, behind those eyes that remain on us for a long moment, as if great secrets lay upon our eyelids?

A hidden heart, a soul, its secret crises, its outbursts, its despairs, the desires of the body and its indelible decline, the sorrows that are so difficult to hide or guess at, the uncertain and troubled struggle towards happiness, is the great drama of man.

But there too is the real revolution: bringing light to spirits caught in the shadows; to aid in the restoration of failing souls; to relearn that we consist of more than just a body; to perfect the imperfect; to rise to heights of virtue, no matter how great the efforts required of us.

This revolution alone can be enchanting — but terrifying.

We all walk through a labyrinth.

That thin bowed head and that beautiful golden hair, that laughter that bursts too suddenly, that arm that descends? Ten faces, ten abysses.

Who cheats us? Who is mistaken? Who seeks to deceive us?

We only see the deceptive shadows of beings. Everyone tries to deceive themselves, to deceive others, by simplifications and by more or less skillful artifices.

And it is among these subterfuges, however, that we must advance, our flames burning white in the darkest night!

What is there to take hold of?

What can we do about these beings who to our impotent eyes appear only as mysteries, mysteries all the more poignant as we observe their laughter, vivacious eyes, pale foreheads, this soft caress of flowing hair, which with joyful light oppose all our regrets, anguish, weariness, and corruptions!

We all make our way along distant paths. The bottoms of our hearts alone know our true face, the false secrets of our soul, its hopes and faults, our true joys and our true sorrows.

There were so many joys and so many tears that the others thought they knew, shared, or assuaged... We look, in the hours of solitude, at our real selves, where no one else, alas, can ever go. This inner self tells us who he loves, and to whom he belongs, what overwhelms him and causes him to stumble, and tells us what raises up his spirit, perhaps, if by fortune, the breath of truth brushes aside this invisible veil.

To be this current, this great warm and long wind which rises from the depths of our spiritual horizons, which gives souls this first movement...

All of a sudden, the sail undergoes an impalpable swelling, rounding off in the light.

The hull slips across still waters.

The inflection of the white sails gently pushes the air away.

We think of those thousands of motionless sails waiting for what will give them, imperceptibly at first, then with quivering force, life and movement, the joy of moving through air and water, advancing towards the clear line of the horizon in the distance...

The boats are heavy. The water is dark and sluggish.

Everything is silent.

Be this breath that will come at last to rouse these souls, to push them off, clumsy at first, left after so much waiting and stagnation, then happy and firm as the strength that sustains them and the life that revives them is confirmed, show all these beings that existence can be beautiful, and pure, and great, even after all the weaknesses and all the disenchantments, to bring up, from these dry, or numb, or perverted hearts, the fountain of renewal: this is the task, the real one, the hard one, the necessary task...

Terrible task!

We would like to take these half-dead people in our arms, look deeply into their eyes, ward off these creeping doubts and hesitations, to run our trembling fingers through their silken hair.

But what a stir upon meeting those eyes which return the light of others, those eyes which show us so quickly, from their first lie, or their first confession, the confusion that inhabits us ourselves!

How to look at a face without hearing cruel questions? Are you lying? How shall you fare under fire, under privations of the flesh? And what will remain tomorrow of the hopes and aspirations, painfully suspended, buoyed by this gaze?

The source of all redemption lies there, however: to give life to drifting souls, to calm the storms which break their masts and tear their sails, to give them sun and breath, to make serene the seas of men, to make their horizon clear, free from the shadows and perils of violent and tormented skies...

Breathe... Resume believing in virtues, in beauty, in goodness, in love...

Feel dancing around you, on the waves, a thousand other sails, full of wind, carried with the same momentum towards the same call...

When the golden sea sees these white sails rush forth, the Revolution will be on its way, carried onwards by this flotilla of souls.

XXXIII – Summits

Your road is hard.

You come short of breath. There are times when you would like to throw away this burden that weighs you down, let yourself go downhill and return to those idyllic farms that welcome you back at the bottom of the hill, blue streams against the green and gray backgrounds of meadows and slate roofs.

You feel nostalgic for the quiet waters and the clear rushes, the oar that laps against the surface, the flat, effortless path along the banks. You would like to think of nothing, wash away the memories of men from your thoughts and, with your back against the grass, watch the passing sky, lightened by the flocks of birds.

No more weariness! You won't let go of your bag and your stick! You won't attend to your bleeding knees! You won't listen to the clamor of hatred; you won't look at the smiling eyes and the wickedness they hide! It is to the summit that you must cast your eyes! Your body should live only for these twisting paths, your heart should dream only of those heights that you and the others should reach.

What lies at the root of your confusion? You thought you would find immediate joys in climbing this path along the sea, in raising this human host. You have often suffered. Sometimes you feel nauseous. Yet you needed it. You had to learn that ambition does not pay off, that sooner or later it tires out the heart it possesses. You know it now. You know that you should not expect any constant joy from outside; you have learned to doubt the comfort of men; your face is flushed, not from the tenderness they gave you, but from the blows that you were dealt by them.

Of course, you did not think it would. You imagined that along the road your hands and eyes would find what you so feverishly desired.

You look back.

And you say: I am going back down.

No; It is only then that life becomes noble, when it beats you down, when you no longer have the enthusiasm to carry on.

Do you remember the early days? You wanted a beautiful climb; it is true. You were leaving this way to free your soul. You knew that man must always overcome his limitations! Didn't you believe in this obscure pleasure of honor and discipline?

Are you crying out?

You did not think for it to be like this. You rejected comfort with sincere enough words. But it still hemmed the edge of your actions, as the foam borders the edge of the sea. You honestly thought that you only lived for this thread of light, beautiful only from afar, on the edge of the sands. The temptation was there in your heart. You wanted something grand, something real. But you still had the thought of yourself near you. You announced your readiness to do your duty. But you made this silent addition, that to fulfill your duty would bring glory to your name and satisfy your own desires, would make you golden with pride!

It is because you don't see this phantasm before you anymore that your eyes reflect only shadows. You are looking in the dark.

Confront it, the fact that you loved something false.

Those who have disgusted you a hundred times, with their wickedness and injustice, have carried you more than your own strength.

Are you giving up? You give your flesh and your breath, your heart and your mind, and you think now it is all in vain?

In vain? Why, because you no longer give them in service of your selfish pride?

Only now can you start to give of yourself.

That wickedness had to overwhelm you. By the time you were almost fainting, at the end of your effort, the jeers would rise, and contempt would drive you on.

It was necessary that all your gestures of love be covered with hatred, that all your impulses be soiled, that each throbbing of your heart command a new blow to fall upon your face...

You have known, so many times, those exhausting last few meters where you smiled on the threshold of the goal, despite your sweat and your pallor: the next moment, you were falling among the rocks, betrayed by your own, overwhelmed by the others. Everything had to be redone.

And always the charming emptiness of the valley below hailed you, the trembling poplars called you like a line of ships on the sea of easy days.

You suffered from the harshness of the fighting. You said to yourself: whatever the victory, the price is too expensive, and I no longer desire it.

You always thought of yourself. Yes, for you, for the human pleasure of having reached the top, you made a fool's bargain. But if life had not slapped you a hundred times, would you ever have understood that there are other pleasures than pride, than smiles, than glory?

You have felt the hypocrisy of so many faces around you! You have guessed all the lies, all the gall, all the meanness that is in store for you, every time you start climbing again.

Part Six: To Give Completely

You are no longer entitled to anything.

You hear the swarm of slithering horrors. You know you will go through with the abjection anyways.

It is at the hour when you have given everything that you will be said to be greedy.

It is at the hour when your heart will suffer the most abandonment that it will be given the basest of demands.

You turn around with tears that well up in spite of you. Why? Are you still thinking of yourself?

Do you still suffer from injustice, is it all about you?

How hard it is to be free from our humanity!

Let them come crashing down on your life like jackals, let them trample your dreams, let them open your heart to all the winds!

Suffer from being thrown to the beasts of envy, calumny, baseness! Endure, above all — and this is what bruises the most — that at the moment when you cannot take it any longer, when your knees bend, when your eyes cast about for a supportive look, your arms search for an ardent hand, support, while you are hanging on a word, a look, that this word falls down to break you, that look to hurt you; accept that it is those who were closest to you who finish you off, those to whom you had left everything, whom you loved so naively, without reserve and without hesitation…

Your eyes have a bewilderment worse than tears! Do not cry out. Expect that everything you suffered yesterday, tomorrow will be renewed. Accept this in advance. Do not even turn around when you hear that step behind your back. Bless the blows received. Love those who will bring them.

They are more useful to you than a thousand hearts that love you.

Did you get it?

You may find tomorrow, or perhaps you have found already, that tenderness that comes to you like a breath of fresh air, or like the scent of a cluster of country flowers.

You are now without weakness in front of them.

You will only enjoy dignity to the extent that, by dint of suffering, you have learned to do without it.

This you would never have obtained, had you not paid the price hundreds of times, without ever being sure of receiving anything in return.

If one day this appears to you, enjoy it as a sublime landscape glimpsed in passing. But it is not for this that you came: it is the air; it is the light of the summits calling you! You are breathing better already. You will slowly attain true joy, at those great peaks of consciousness, shining, unsullied. Think only of this, see only this, try to get there, light, pure, radiant with sunlight.

It is your weaknesses and your faults on which you should weigh; on them alone; your pride, your name, the vain appeals of the departing man, throw them beyond the rocks!

Part Six: To Give Completely

Did you hear them break, as they bounced down the slope? May it all perish! May bitterness and abandonment, instead of rebellion, keep you on the path! These two howling dogs are the guardians of the herd of your thoughts. Without them you would stop, you would pull away. Do not waste a moment. It is far. And you must reach the summit.

When you reach these pure immensities, behind you will be a great silence. All those who screamed after you, who hated or trampled you despite the smiles on their faces, all those who, just to strike at you, followed you on the road, will suddenly realize that at this game they have, they too reached the snows, the new air, and the horizons cut out in the sky. They will forget to hate you. They will have wonderfully childish eyes. They will discover the essential. Their souls will have been lifted to heights they would never have agreed to reach if your back that received their blows had not hidden the length of the road.

So you will have it, your victory! You will be able, having given the final effort, suddenly to fall, arms outstretched, from the top of the mountain into the rocks below.

You will be done.

You will have won. Reaching the end of your own journey by the last effort will no longer matter if the others are there, on the brink of the pure immensities of redemption.

You are so happy, deep down.

You know the only happiness is there.

Sing!

May your voice thunder in the valleys!

Regrets and tears? The most unremarkable man among you all has suffered this, and you would reject him?

The hardest thing is done. Hold on. Clench your teeth. Silence your heart. Think only of the top! Go up!